Enchantment of the World

BRUNEI

By David K. Wright

Consultant for Brunei: Allen R. Maxwell, Ph.D., Associate Professor, Department of Anthropology, The University of Alabama, Tuscaloosa

Consultant for Reading: Robert L. Hillerich, Ph.D., Visiting Professor, University of South Florida; Consultant, Pinellas County Schools, Florida

CHILDRENS PRESS®
CHICAGO

Almost half of the population of Brunei is under the age of twenty.

Library of Congress Cataloging-in-Publication Data

Wright, David K.
  Brunei / by David K. Wright.
    p.   cm. — (Enchantment of the world)
  Includes index.
  Summary: An introduction to the small and prosperous country of Brunei, which lies on the north coast of the island of Borneo.
  ISBN 0-516-02602-X
  1. Brunei—Juvenile literature. [1. Brunei.]
I. Title. II. Series.
DS650.3.W75 1991   91-22511
959.55—dc20   CIP
                                          AC

Picture Acknowledgments
AP/Wide World Photos: 35, 36 (2 photos), 37, 38, 65 (2 photos)
© **John Elk III:** 70, 84 (2 photos), 88 (right), 101 (top and bottom right)
© **Victor Englebert:** 12 (right), 41 (inset), 46, 47, 85, 86, 87 (bottom), 88 (left), 89, 100 (left), 102, 107 (left and bottom right)

H. Armstrong Roberts: © **Charles Phelps Cushing,** 34
Historical Pictures Service, Chicago: 30, 32, 54
North Wind Picture Archives: 26 (inset), 29, 33
Photri: 8, 9, 10 (top right), 12 (left), 24, 41, 43, 48, 59, 60, 61, 66, 73, 75, 76, 77, 99, 103, 104, 106; © **Fovea,** 42, 45, 51, 52 (2 photos), 55, 74, 80 (top), 83, 90, 93, 97, 109; © **George Hunter,** 72 (bottom), 82
© **Ann Purcell:** 10 (bottom), 96
© **Carl Purcell:** 13, 100 (right), 101 (left)
Root Resources: © **Mary Ann Hemphill,** 50 (right), 107 (top right); © **Jane P. Downton,** 80 (bottom); © **Bryan Hemphill,** 122
Tom Stack & Associates: © **Mark Newman,** 14 (bottom right), 18, 20 (left), 21 (left); © **Gary Milburn,** 16; © **David Barker,** 17; © **Larry Tackett,** 48 (inset); © **Nancy Adams,** 14 (top); © **Thomas Kitchin,** 14 (bottom left)
SuperStock International, Inc.: © **World Photo Service,** 72 (top), 79; © **Joe Barnell,** 78; © **Robin Smith,** 87 (top); © **David Warren,** 110
TSW-CLICK/Chicago: © **Marcus Brooke,** Cover; © **Jim Olive,** 4, 5, 6 (bottom), 23, 26, 50 (left), 108; © **David Leake Jr.,** 22, 94; © **Nabel Turner,** 57
Valan: © **Kennon Cooke,** 20 (right); © **Joyce Photographics,** 21 (right)
Len W. Meents: Maps on 71, 73, 85
Courtesy Flag Research Center, Winchester, Massachusetts 01890: Flag on back cover
Cover: Kampung Ayer, water village; Bandar Seri Begawan Mosque

Actors in a Chinese theater performance

TABLE OF CONTENTS

*Right: Brunei's flag
Below: An aerial view
of Bandar Seri Begawan,
the capital of Brunei,
with Kampung Ayer
in the foreground*

Chapter 1

ABODE OF PEACE

A flag says a lot about a country. The flag of Brunei is yellow with two diagonal stripes, one black and one white. This simple and attractive flag was created in 1906, when Brunei was a British protectorate and life was far different from what it is today. Today Brunei, on the island of Borneo, is a modern state and a member of the United Nations, the Association of Southeast Asian Nations (ASEAN), the British Commonwealth of Nations, and the Organization of Islam Conference.

The state motto was added to the flag in 1949. It is written in Arabic script and says, "Always render service by God's guidance." Religion is quite important to Brunei residents. Most are Muslims—people who follow the religion of Islam—despite the fact that they live thousands of miles from the Middle East where Islam began.

The flag became more complicated with the addition of the state crest in 1959. A symbol for Brunei coronations since the fifteenth century, the bright red crest includes a small flag and a royal umbrella. Just below these are wings of four feathers, the feathers representing justice, tranquility, prosperity, and peace. A hand on either side stands for the government's pledge to promote wealth,

Offshore oil and gas production facility

peace, and prosperity. A large crescent represents Islam, the state religion. And the scroll at the bottom of the crest reads, "Brunei Darussalam, Abode of Peace." Just as the flag grew more complex, so did Bruneian life in the twentieth century because of the discovery of oil.

"BLACK GOLD" COMES TO BRUNEI

Brunei today is peaceful and incredibly prosperous. The discovery of oil in the late 1920s, followed by the finding of large amounts of oil offshore in the 1960s, has resulted in one of the highest standards of living in Southeast Asia. The oil is recovered offshore, refined in Brunei and Malaysia, and then sold worldwide.

The resulting avalanche of money has made Brunei a welfare state. Medical care is free. Education is free, whether a citizen

*A water taxi passes dense jungle as
it journeys down one of Brunei's many rivers.*

attends an elementary school in the capital of Bandar Seri
Begawan or studies abroad in an American or English university.
There is no income tax. The government gives generous pensions
to the elderly and disabled. People who live in substandard
housing are offered land, farm animals, money to start over, and a
new home—free of charge. People work for their living, but there
is no poverty. Life is good and people pattern their lives to fit with
the hot, humid climate.

About one-fifth of Brunei's citizens live in Bandar Seri Begawan,
the nation's capital. Many are employed by the government.
Bandar Seri Begawan sparkles with huge new government office
buildings. Other Bruneians live in smaller coastal towns that serve
the vast offshore oil-drilling operations. Still others live in fishing
villages or operate small farms, though the harvest from farming
does not come close to meeting the country's food needs. Up the
country's numerous rivers live several thousand people whose
fathers and grandfathers may have been headhunters.

Faces of Brunei

The majority of Bruneians, about 65 percent, are of Malay descent, and about 20 percent trace their ancestry back to mainland China. There are about 8 percent indigenous people—the Muruts, Tutongs, Belaits, Penans, and Ibans—and 6 percent who are temporary residents involved in oil production and related businesses.

TOPOGRAPHY AND CLIMATE

Brunei is a very small country with four districts. It is all that remains of a kingdom that ruled this part of the South China Sea on the western edge of the Pacific some five hundred years ago. The country has swamps and wide beaches, and 75 percent of the country is heavily forested. Some of the things Brunei does *not* share with other Southeast Asian countries are volcanoes, and the earthquakes and tidal waves that accompany them.

Hills are found inland, but even the highest is far too low and too near the equator to ever have frost or snow on its peaks. The average year-round temperature is about 82 degrees Fahrenheit (28 degrees Celsius), with rain every day for five months and occasional showers the rest of the year.

THE PEOPLE OF BRUNEI

Malay people today are found from Singapore through Indonesia and into Malaysia. Most speak more or less the same language—Malay—are Muslims, and, historically, have farmed, fished, and traded while living simply in small villages. Today Malays fill almost all of Brunei's governmental positions. Two of every three Bruneians are Malay.

11

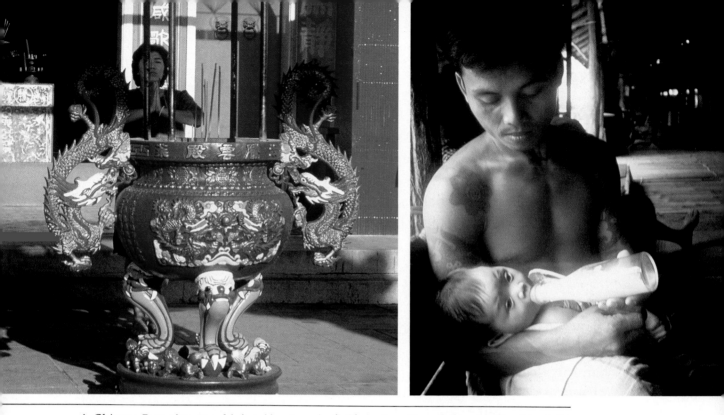

A Chinese Bruneian worshiping in a temple (left) and an Iban father feeding his child

If the Malays run the country, the small but vital number of people of Chinese descent make it hum with activity. These hardworking people can be found in two-story shop houses, where their business is on the ground floor and their (usually large) families live behind and above the business establishment. The business may involve small-engine repair or a restaurant. Whether at work squatting on the pavement in front of a store or behind a big desk in one of the capital's shiny new office buildings, Chinese Bruneians are intensely involved in commerce.

The indigenous people, the Muruts and Ibans, live along the rivers, sometimes in longhouses, where an entire village may exist under one roof. Wiry, tough, and friendly, these tribespeople are eager to make the adjustment to modern life without abandoning the jungle traditions that have made them admired and feared by visitors down through history.

One means of transportation is the water taxi.

MODERN-DAY PROSPERITY

About 95 percent of the young people can read, which puts Brunei among the most literate nations on earth. Schools offer every modern convenience and teachers are well trained.

There are approximately fifty thousand television sets, seventy-five thousand radios, and thirty-five thousand telephones in Brunei. The government-run television service has been all color since 1975. There are two radio stations, one broadcasting in Malay and the other in Chinese. Almost every family owns at least one shiny, new Japanese car.

With many hospitals and a modern nurses' training center, the country provides more than adequate free medical care. Life expectancy is a healthy seventy-four years, despite the danger of tropical diseases, the large number of cars on the country's highway system, and boats buzzing up and down rivers.

Bruneians like their country, its government, and the many modern conveniences. It is an ideal place to live. For at least as long as there is oil beneath its offshore waters, Brunei should continue to be a land of plenty.

The aptly-named proboscis monkey (above), and a sun bear (below left) Macaques (below right) are mammals related to monkeys.

Chapter 2

A SMALL COUNTRY
ON A LARGE ISLAND

Borneo is the world's third-largest island—only Greenland and New Guinea are bigger. Technically Australia is the largest island, but it is classified as a continent. Thousands of years ago, Borneo probably was joined to the Asian mainland by a land bridge. Then the glaciers melted and the oceans rose, but not before thousands of different kinds of birds, animals, insects, and, perhaps, primitive people made the island of Borneo their home. Today, some animals that are extinct or endangered in Asia still exist on Borneo. They share wild, inland areas with primitive hunters, nomads, and farmers.

THE WORLD'S RAREST ANIMAL?

Somewhere on this island shared by Brunei, Malaysia, and Indonesia there are probably a few rhinoceroses. These animals were thought for years to be extinct, but one of the Borneo rhinos was sighted and photographed in the deep jungle. The chubby, foul-tempered beasts were hunted for centuries by local people with spears and by foreigners with guns. Now, they are rare and protected.

Other mammals well known on Borneo include the shy orangutan whose name means "man of the forest," monkeys such

Some shrews weigh only .07 ounce (2 grams)—less than a U.S. dime.

as langurs, gibbons, and macaques, long-clawed sun bears, honey bears, deer, wild cats, wild pigs, rats, mice, bats, squirrels, and shrews. The largest numbers of these mammals are rats and mice, bats, and squirrels. Shrews look a bit like mice. One species of shrew has found a great way to protect itself: it gives off a terrible smell that drives away animals and people. Those who have been downwind from this stinky shrew claim the smell is much worse than a North American skunk.

Down the food chain a notch are the reptiles. The largest are the crocodiles, who are found in both salt water and fresh water. Also found in salt and fresh water are hard and soft-shelled turtles. The saltwater turtles tend to be larger; some have shells as big around as car tires. Some saltwater turtles swim through hundreds of miles of ocean water each year to return to their home beaches to lay eggs. There are lizards in many sizes, from the large water monitor to the tiny gecko.

A young cat snake

THE SNAKE POPULATION

In contrast to dozens of kinds of harmless frogs and toads, some snakes present possible danger. There are 166 kinds of snakes on the island. Two types of cobra, two kraits, the green pit vipers, and two kinds of coral snakes live in Brunei and the nearby waters and are very dangerous. Unusual snakes include mock vipers, Malayan racers, whip snakes, and cat snakes. Hamadryads or king cobras are deadly poisonous snakes that should be avoided.

BIRDS

Both harmless and beautiful are the island's birds. Many magnificent species are visible simply by parking the car or

stopping the boat and looking across a field or into the jungle canopy. Fish eagles, black eagles, kingfishers, trillers, kites, birds of paradise, broadbills, hornbills, flycatchers, herons, sandpipers, swifts, pheasants, shrikes, orioles, and dozens more rare and familiar birds are found all over the island. The smallest owl in Borneo is the Pygmy owlet—six inches (fifteen centimeters) tall. Quite simply, this may be the best place on earth to watch birds.

The many birds have big appetites. Food is plentiful, thanks to the many plants and the incredible number of insects all about. Wherever you travel, noisy cicadas hum and whir. Cockroaches fly and scurry along, equally at home on the jungle floor or in a bathroom sink. There are thousands of different kinds of beetles. Termite nests are everywhere. Even though flies and mosquitoes are snacks for many reptiles and birds, they continue to show up in large numbers.

Wormlike leeches that live on a diet of blood attach themselves to humans and animals. One type is as thin as thread and lives in stream water. Others drop onto passersby as they walk in the dense undergrowth. They make a painless bite and then hang on and swell as they suck blood from the unaware victim, be it human or beast.

Not all of the creatures are annoying: hundreds of species of butterflies, some with wingspans of seven inches (eighteen centimeters) or more, flash and flutter. They make even the thickest jungle come alive with color.

The most dangerous animals in Borneo are bees and wasps—far more dangerous than poisonous snakes or crocodiles.

Opposite page: A great variety of insects and birds live in the treetops and dense undergrowth of Brunei's jungles.

Brunei is 75 percent forest (left); hibiscus blooms (right)

FIVE KINDS OF FOREST

Five kinds of forests cover about three-quarters of Brunei. They are mangrove, heath (shrub-covered), peat swamp, mixed, and mountainous. The original and untouched tropical rain forest is thick with trees that are two hundred feet (sixty-one meters) high, living on the poor soil. The trees—and the plants that exist amid their leaves and branches—shut out much of the blazing, equatorial sun or even the hardest rain.

Secondary jungle grows on land that has been burned or otherwise cleared. It features smaller, faster-growing trees, plus bushes, creepers, and ferns. Logging, which removes valuable hardwoods from the jungles, is carefully regulated in Brunei. Half of all forests have been designated state preserves. With two seasons, hot and wet and hot and occasionally wet, many areas are thick with the aromas of flowering plants and shrubs during much of the year.

Above: Durians are delicious fruit, despite their pungent smell.
Left: A pitcher plant

Fruit is important for the local diet, in part because it grows easily in the warm climate. Fruit trees include coconut, guava, and jackfruit. The durian, a tree with a strong-smelling fruit that tastes like a delicious custard, is a favorite. Wild fruit abounds in the forests of Borneo.

The world's largest flower, 3 feet (.9 meter) wide, grows only on the island of Borneo and it, too, has a strong smell. Called the rafflesia, this fat, stinky flower grows deep in the jungle on the roots of other plants.

Flowers bloom everywhere. Orchids dangle from jungle vines and hibiscus blooms nod in the tropical breezes. There are several varieties of pitcher plants, flowers that get their nutrition by trapping insects. Ants and other bugs are lured inside the flower by a sweet, sticky substance. The insects become trapped and the plant slowly digests them. Escape is difficult, since the walls of the flower are slick and tiny thorns ring the edge of the plant.

Travel through the forests and jungle can be done in water in a

Tropical vegetation grows to the river's edge.

shallow boat or on land by following narrow human or animal trails. Rivers and streams rise and fall quickly whenever there is rain. High water covers boulders and logs and makes upstream travel difficult and dangerous. Walking in the jungle is possible with a *parang,* a long broad knife similar to a machete, which is used by natives to hack through or past shrubs and vines.

The trails can be slick and muddy in the rainy season, even though tree leaves and shaggy vines keep sun or rain off. Hikers tell about meeting a jungle dweller staggering home under the weight of a large bag of salt or coffee, carried from the nearest store miles away. Sometimes travelers might meet a dangerous sun bear or a snorting wild pig.

Fishermen sort their catch

VARIETIES OF FISH

The rivers teem with freshwater fish such as puthihan and haruan, which are used for food. They provide an important source of protein for inland residents, who spear plump fish in stream eddies. Bruneians living on the coast and in the capital city enjoy eating ocean fish, shrimp and other shellfish, prawns, and eels. Offshore oil-drilling platforms shelter a wide variety of ocean fish, from tasty grouper to schools of huge sharks.

THE LAND

Brunei is on Borneo's northwest coast. It is a tiny place, just 2,226 square miles (5,765 square kilometers) in area. That is about the size of the state of Delaware. The coastline is 100 miles (161 kilometers) long. Coastal Brunei is either thick with twisted mangrove trees or has smooth and sandy beaches.

An aerial view of an interior river, showing
a typical tropical lowland meander stream pattern.

The country is bounded on the north by the South China Sea and on all other sides by the Malaysian state of Sarawak. Sarawak also divides Brunei into two parts. The northeastern part is the district of Temburong. The larger, northwestern area consists of the districts of Brunei-Muara, Tutong, and Belait.

The land developed on ancient bedrock and is made up of sandstone, shale, and clay. There are several rivers. The rivers of Temburong District flow into Brunei Bay and the rivers of the other districts flow northward into the South China Sea. The western part of the country is hilly lowland, rising to heights of about 985 feet (300 meters). In the east, the wide coastal plain reaches up to a height of 6,040 feet (1,841 meters) above sea level at a point far inland named *Bukit Pagon*, "Pagon Mountain." In the jungle, trees are continually being recycled as dead trees nourish new growth.

HOT AND WET

The tropical climate makes Brunei hot all year round. The temperatures range from 73 degrees to 89 degrees Fahrenheit (22.7 degrees to 31.6 degrees Celsius). The relative humidity is between 67 percent and 91 percent. Fungus is a problem and even stainless steel can rust.

Yearly rainfall ranges from 109 inches (277 centimeters) in the lowland areas to more than 143 inches (363 centimeters) in parts of the interior, although in some years, there have been more than 200 inches (508 centimeters) of rain. Periods of heaviest rain usually run from November through March each year. During these months, it rains every day. Showers also occur in other months, but not like the rainy season, when showers start and stop at almost the same time every afternoon.

Brunei is exactly halfway around the world from Columbia, the country in the northwest corner of South America. Only 270 miles (434 kilometers) north of the equator, Brunei is eleven hours ahead of New York City and Montreal. So when it is midnight Monday in New York City, it is 11 A.M. Tuesday in Brunei.

BRUNEI'S NEIGHBORS

Brunei's neighbors across the South China Sea are Singapore and mainland Malaysia to the west; Thailand, Cambodia, and Vietnam to the northwest; Hong Kong and mainland China directly north; and Taiwan and the Philippine Islands to the northeast. The closest neighbors are the Malaysian states of Sarawak and Sabah. They share the island of Borneo with Kalimantan, which is part of Indonesia.

Chinese traders came to
Brunei in boats called
junks (left). The capital,
Bandar Seri Begawan,
is situated on the
Brunei River, which
empties into Brunei Bay.

Chapter 3

AN OCEAN VIEW

Who were the world's first ocean sailors? No one knows. Perhaps they were the early sailors of the Mediterranean or perhaps they were the early Southeast Asians who went from island to island on their way to Australia, more than forty thousand years ago.

Probably the earliest long-distance, open-ocean sailors were the ancestors of the people who inhabit the distant islands in the Pacific Ocean.

About fifteen hundred years ago, Chinese sailors came to Brunei, which they called Puni or Poli. The Chinese arrived too late to meet the first people in Brunei who were no longer there. Little is known of these people who used stone tools and hunted with spears. They left evidence of their existence for archaeologists to discover, such as the burial of their dead in a cave.

When the Chinese arrived in Brunei to trade, they found a wealthy coastal kingdom. The people in this kingdom grew rice and traded with people who lived in inland areas.

The Chinese were interested in trading products that their country produced—porcelain and brass ware—for items that could not be found in their homeland. Among the most important items were hornbill casques (helmets), feathers, and resins. Centuries later a pepper trade developed. Records indicate numerous Chinese visits to Brunei from about A.D. 500.

WHERE PIRATES ROAMED

Sailors and traders from other nations visited Brunei later, but the north coast of Borneo soon became notorious for its pirates. From the Philippines through Indonesia to Burma, tough wiry men sailed small, fast boats that could overtake the ships of most other countries. These Bajaus, Bugis, Sudanese, Sumatrans, or Thais captured boats and killed or enslaved crew members. The pirates hid from military expeditions amid the thousands of Indonesian and Philippine islands. Even today, unprotected yachts and other smaller, oceangoing vessels are at risk from pirates in this part of the world.

Adventurous Indian Muslims began to trade in Borneo a few centuries after the Chinese. The early kingdoms in Borneo used alphabets brought from India for their writing. But the Muslim traders introduced the Arabic alphabet. The Jawi alphabet is the Arabic alphabet with a few new letters added from Persian so that it can be used for writing Malay or Indonesian. When the Europeans arrived in Brunei in 1521, the Brunei Malays were using the Jawi alphabet for all their writing.

Chinese accounts from the Ming Dynasty report that Islam reached Brunei sometime before A.D. 1371. Awang Alak Betatar, Brunei's first ruler, became a Muslim and changed his name to

A woodcut shows Europeans, who came in search of spices that grew near the island of Borneo.

Sultan Muhammad when he married a Malayan woman.

A series of *sultans*, Muslim sovereigns, ruled Brunei in the following centuries. They were all members of the same family— today's sultan is their direct descendant. These powerful men spread their influence while fellow Muslims spread the religion. The Brunei leaders who most successfully acquired wealth and power were the fifth and ninth sultans in the line—Bolkiah and Hassan. They subdued pirates and profited from trade, creating a small empire.

EUROPEAN VISITORS

European contact began in A.D. 1521. The Portuguese were especially interested in the spices that grew in the Moluccas, a group of small islands southeast of Borneo, between Sulawesi and New Guinea. A Portuguese adventurer named Ferdinand Magellan, sailing from Seville in 1519 on behalf of the king of

A steel engraving from the early 1800s of Ferdinand Magellan, who sailed for the king of Spain, trying to find the East Indies.

Spain, attempted to reach the fabled East Indies by pointing his five ships west from Europe. He and 240 sailors crossed the Atlantic Ocean and rounded the southern tip of South America. Magellan continued westward across the Pacific with three ships. Five ships had set out, but only one returned to Spain. The sailors ran out of food and water on the long Pacific crossing. They told tales of being so hungry that they ate much of the leather used to tie things together on board. Finally, they landed on the island of Guam after ninety-nine days without fresh food.

Magellan led his ships toward the Philippines. He wanted to restock before visiting the Spice Islands. In early 1521, he claimed an area of the Philippines for Spain and converted the people to Christianity. But on Mactan Island, which was under the control of the sultan of Brunei, the Portuguese and Spanish sailors fought a battle with natives. Magellan was killed on April 27, 1521. The sailors continued, visiting the Moluccas and Brunei itself. Antonio Pigafetta, the chronicler of the Magellan voyage, was the first

European to visit Brunei and record his observations for posterity. But only one ship, heavy with rich spices, was able to limp westward around India and Africa. Just 18 men survived this first trip around the world.

The Portuguese were followed to the Southeast Asian islands by the Spanish, the Dutch, and the French. The Spanish conquered the Philippines and named it after Philip, one of their kings. The Dutch ruled all of what is known today as Indonesia. The French established outposts in India and along the coast of Vietnam.

The British were somewhat late in arriving in this part of the world, but they quickly made up for lost time. They chased the Portuguese out of India and the Malay Peninsula and established the cities of Singapore and Hong Kong. Much of this work was done not by the British government but by independent British adventurers. One such person was James Brooke.

THE BROOKE REIGN

Brooke, who lived in India, was the son of a British businessman. He served as a soldier along the Indian frontier, fighting bravely to keep the big subcontinent under English control. After being wounded in Burma, he used money he inherited to buy a ship. With a small crew, he sailed in 1838 from India east into the South China Sea. Brooke and his crew landed in Sarawak, on Borneo's north coast, just as Malay chieftains in the area were rebelling against a relative of the sultan of Brunei. The Englishman used his peacemaking powers—and the threat of cannons—to end the dispute. He further amazed both sides by refusing to execute anyone.

For his efforts at peacemaking, the sultan gave Brooke the state

The Government House in Sarawak, from a wood engraving of 1864 published in the Illustrated London News

of Sarawak, perhaps one-third of the sultan's kingdom at the time. Brooke was only thirty-eight when he was crowned *rajah*, "ruler." Rajah comes from the Sanskrit word *raja* that means "king." The North Borneo Company of England also took control of the state of Sabah at about the same time. So the size of Brunei was reduced drastically.

The Brooke family may have been odd, but they were all completely honest. Even though they ruled Sarawak with absolute authority, James Brooke and his successors were often strapped for money. They were a colorful bunch; one of James Brooke's descendants wore a glass eye that had come from a stuffed owl in a taxidermy shop.

The British in Sabah (called North Borneo at the time) also were quite honest, trading with local people in a way that made England wealthy without stripping the land and the people of all value. Nevertheless, there was discrimination based on race. Most

The USS Constitution *was the first ship from the United States to visit Brunei. This engraving appeared in* Harper's Monthly *in 1892.*

Englishmen were discouraged from socializing with the locals, although the Brooke clan violated this unwritten rule on a regular basis.

DEVELOPMENT LAGS

In general British development was slow on Borneo for several reasons. The island was almost impenetrable due to thick forests, dense swamps, walls of rain, intense heat, and terrible diseases. The British were content to exploit mainland Malaysia, where they created thriving rubber and palm oil industries and mined tin. A few logging operations did well on Borneo, where there were large stands of valuable hardwood trees.

In 1845, the USS *Constitution*, paid a visit to Brunei. The U.S. and Brunei signed a treaty of friendship and cooperation in 1850 and the two countries have been on friendly terms since then.

The Suez Canal opened in 1869.

Relations were further solidified in 1864 when America's Charles Lee Moses opened a United States consulate in Brunei. Moses wanted to be another white rajah, like James Brooke, but failed.

The opening of the Suez Canal in Egypt in 1869 brought Europeans to Southeast Asia in greater numbers. In the late nineteenth and early twentieth centuries the British explored Borneo, mapping coastal areas and meeting many different tribespeople. Brunei had been reduced by this time to its current size and in 1888 the country became a British protectorate. At about the same time, a few Chinese immigrants landed and began trading such things as shotgun shells, salt, sugar, pottery, implements, and simple appliances for treasures from the island's little-known interior. Other active traders in the area were the Bugis from the nearby Sulawesi (Celebes) Islands to the east.

Progress came slowly to Brunei during the first forty years of the twentieth century, although modern products from Britain and other countries continued to arrive and to be highly prized.

Destruction on the island of Borneo from World War II

On the political front, the British continued to advise the sultan. The British left matters such as problems over Malayan customs or religion to the Bruneians. In many other parts of the British Empire, such as India and Burma, local people were questioning English rule. But in Brunei, life continued peacefully.

WORLD WAR II AND ITS AFTERMATH

The discovery of oil in Seria, Brunei, in 1929, made living conditions more prosperous and comfortable. But the relaxed, tropical life-style was changed by World War II. In early 1942 the entire northern coast of Borneo fell to the Japanese. For more than three years, British citizens were imprisoned or killed and native Bruneians were abused by Japanese, who needed oil and other raw materials from this part of the world to help in their war effort.

English, Canadian, American, and Australian prisoners of war suffered and died on Borneo. Clothing rotted off the sweating

Above: Sukarno, Indonesian dictator, advised the Japanese during World War II. He was noted for his forceful and dynamic speeches. Left: Captured Indonesians sit on the floor of a truck as Malaysian troops take them to a police station.

bodies of prisoners and both prisoners and the Bruneians were malnourished. Iban warriors from the interior killed and beheaded Japanese soldiers to keep the invaders out of the island interior. The Japanese left when Japan surrendered in August 1945.

After the Japanese departed, Communists developed an interest in British Malaya and Indonesia. Because of a Muslim distrust of communism and a long-standing friendship with Great Britain, Brunei stopped a Communist takeover.

In 1957 British Malaya became self-governing Malaysia without Brunei's participation. Later, in 1963, the residents of the small, oil-rich nation of Brunei declined to join with Sarawak, Sabah, and Singapore as they became the country of Malaysia.

AVOIDING WAR WITH INDONESIA

Brunei watched nervously in 1962 as Indonesia and the Philippines threatened Malaysian territory with troops. The unrest was created by the Indonesian dictator, Sukarno, who

Sultan Omar Ali Saifuddin

convinced his people, and many Bruneians and Malaysians, that Indonesia had claims to land on the north side of Borneo. Warships cruised Bruneian waters and Indonesian guerrillas sneaked into territory along the island's north coast. Sukarno did little planning; he relied on emotions. The well-organized Malaysians quickly overpowered Indonesian forces that had invaded Sabah and the crisis passed.

Much of the history after World War II is connected to Sultan Omar Ali Saifuddin, who ascended to the throne on the death of his brother in 1950. In 1959 during his reign, a new constitution was written. It declared Brunei a self-governing state, with England looking after Brunei's foreign affairs, security, and defense. The sultan called on British troops in December 1962 to put down a rebellion organized by an opposition political party.

The opposition had won a legal election, but the sultan and his family did not want the winners to take office or share power. The

Sultan Hassanal Bolkiah Mu'izzaddin Waddaulah became the twenty-ninth ruler of Brunei in 1968.

sultan and his relatives claimed that the election winners were part of a plot organized by Indonesia. The British troops and Indian Gurkhas (soldiers) quickly chased down and killed or captured all of the opposition. At peace once again, Sultan Omar Ali Saifuddin began the ambitious public building program that is evident all over the country today.

On October 4, 1967, Sultan Omar Ali Saifuddin abdicated in favor of his eldest son, Sultan Hassanal Bolkiah Mu'izzaddin Waddaulah. The coronation took place on August 1, 1968. In October 1970, the state capital was renamed Bandar Seri Begawan from Brunei Town to honor the Seri Begawan Sultan, former Sultan Omar Ali Saifuddin. Seri Begawan Sultan was one of the sultan's official names.

On January 4, 1979, Sultan Hassanal Bolkiah and the British minister of state signed a new friendship treaty between their two countries. Under the treaty, Brunei was to resume full independence at the end of 1983. On January 1, 1984, Brunei became the fully independent state of Brunei Darussalam.

Chapter 4

AN OIL-BASED ECONOMY

Oil was discovered off the coast of Brunei in 1929. The discovery has changed the country dramatically. The syrupy, brown-black liquid and other substances usually found where there is oil, such as natural gas and tar, have been known to man since ancient times.

Petroleum is needed to make gasoline, engine oil, and dozens of other products. Today, cars in Tokyo, trucks in Europe, construction equipment in Australia, and airplanes in North America rely on Brunei's oil. A bit of oil even finds its way into modern, lifesaving medicines.

Exploring for oil is done by geologists. These people have studied rock formations and searched for oil amid rocks and sand in three ways. They sometimes find likely locations for drilling by studying the earth's surface. Or, they use a seismograph, an instrument that sends sound waves into subsurface rock and tells if there is oil by the ways the echoes bounce back and are recorded on instruments. The third method is to study tiny differences in gravity. A meter can locate large rocks with slight differences in gravity where oil may be hidden. But there is no foolproof way to find deposits of oil, natural gas, and other products.

AN UNDERSEA TREASURE

The geologists who found oil in Brunei faced a tough task. The oil was beneath rock, but much of the rock was off the coast, in the South China Sea. Early Bruneians may have learned of the presence of oil by stepping in tar deposits on beaches or by seeing rainbow-colored smears of oil floating on sea water. The original well was sunk on land, in the town of Seria. But that well hardly compares to today's six offshore oil and gas fields.

The first well-drilling method used a chisel. The chisel chipped away at rocks at the bottom of a hole. Chisels were hung from levers at the surface that moved up and down. This action broke up the rock, but was slow because chisels frequently had to be removed and the broken rock pulled up out of the hole in baskets. As the demand for oil increased worldwide, a better way to drill was invented — the rotary drill.

This improved drill has been used since just before World War II. It rotates as it bores through the rock. Between the drill and the surface, workers keep the drill hole packed with a heavy goo called drilling mud. This messy stuff moves the chipped rock away from the drill by allowing the lighter rock to float up to the surface.

Equally important, drilling mud prevents "gushers," the big squirts of oil seen in old movies, by weighing down the liquid once the drill bit hits a deposit. The mud is fed from a hose down into the hole by a central tube that runs into the drill bit. The many tall derricks, or rigs, seen off Brunei's coast are used to raise and lower drill pipes into wells. At the bottom of the last section of pipe is the rotary drill bit. The drill bit wears out quickly and must be replaced often.

Opposite page: An offshore oil platform and a derrick (inset)

Pipelines carry petroleum to refineries to be refined or purified.

Derricks sit on platforms where the water is less than 200 feet (61 meters) deep. In deeper water the wells are usually drilled from platforms that sit on the bottom of the ocean floor. If the oil lies beneath as much as 2,000 feet (610 meters) of water, a very expensive floating platform is used. With the rotary drill it is possible to drill as deep as 25,000 feet (7,620 meters).

Once oil or gas is hit, the drill is pulled out and a pipe almost as big as the drill hole is inserted. The space between the pipe and the sides of the hole is filled with cement. After additional subsurface equipment is in place, the oil or gas is either pumped or rises naturally due to subsurface pressure. Equipment at the surface takes water and other impurities out of the petroleum.

A PIPELINE OF PROSPERITY

Brunei's most famous product is transported by large pipelines to refineries in Seria in the western section of Brunei or into

A liquefied natural gas plant

Lutong in the Malaysian state of Sarawak. At the refineries the petroleum is refined or purified into a number of different forms. These products include gasoline, aviation gasoline, jet fuel, diesel fuel and oil, other fuel oil, kerosene, lubricating oil, asphalt, and wax.

The refined products leave Brunei or Sarawak in huge tankers and freighters. Brunei keeps track of the flow of petroleum between the wells and the refinery. It charges the oil company, Brunei Shell, a portion of the value of each barrel of oil, plus taxes. That is how the country makes most of its money. The amount of oil extracted off the Brunei coast depends on the worldwide price of crude (unrefined) oil.

Another petroleum product is natural gas. In Brunei natural gas production has exceeded 4.6 million tons (5.08 million metric tons) per year. With more wells being created all the time, and with more efficient ways of recovery, Brunei's petroleum should last only until about the year 2010. But by that time, Bruneians hope to be making money in other ways.

INVESTING OIL MONEY

One of the ways in which the country makes money is by investing its oil fortune in business ventures all over the world. Skyscrapers, housing developments, hotels and other real estate, oceangoing ships, airlines, communications equipment—these and other expensive items in foreign lands are financed by Brunei. The country quietly holds mortgages and loans on such projects. It also owns bonds in governments it feels are stable and will provide a good rate of interest.

In 1988, Brunei and the European Economic Community formed a committee to look into joint business ventures. But not all of Brunei's huge wealth is invested overseas. There are joint ventures underway in Brunei with Shell Oil and with Mitsubishi of Japan in several manufacturing areas.

BUILDING FOR TOMORROW

For its size, Brunei has more new and magnificent public buildings than anywhere on earth. The country's airport can accommodate many more big passenger jets and private carriers than now visit. The post office could process mail as easily as it does today if the population were to double tomorrow. Other new, large, and impressive structures include the ten-story Arts and Handicrafts Training Center, the Supreme Court Building, the

The Supreme Court Building

Legal Department Building, the Brunei Museum, and the Royal
Ceremonial Hall. If the oil ceased flowing tomorrow, Brunei
would not need to add to its public buildings for years.

OTHER EFFORTS

With more than 90 percent of its revenue coming from oil,
Brunei has no immediate need for other economic efforts.
Nevertheless, plans are underway in various fields. One of these is
agriculture. In recent years, the government has introduced
programs to encourage raising livestock and growing rice, fruit,
and vegetables. Experts are at work on increasing the rice yield
and improving its taste. The Sinaut Agriculture Training Center
has been teaching young Bruneians modern farming techniques
since 1976.

Rice growing in a field bordered by private homes

Despite such efforts, oil and natural gas are responsible for 97 percent of Brunei's exports. In one recent year, the country had a trade surplus of 5.18 billion Brunei dollars (about $2.5 billion in United States currency). That means Bruneians sold a great deal more than they purchased from other countries. The country's biggest oil customer is Japan, followed by Thailand, Singapore, the United States, and Taiwan.

A few other products are exported. These include rubber, pepper, and sago. Sago is grown in remote, swampy areas and is used to make sago flour, which is used to make tapioca. People living outside the capital grow rice, yams, peppers, corn, beans, peas, cucumbers, and other vegetables in home gardens.

Water buffalo provide labor as well as meat.

The main source of meat traditionally has been the water buffalo, but epidemics in the mid-1970s greatly reduced herds. Most meat is imported from Australia, with 250 of the 700 cattle that is consumed each month coming from Brunei's own beef-cattle ranch at Willeroo, Northern Territory, in Australia. (This ranch is larger than the whole country of Brunei!) It provides the people of Brunei with 36 percent of their beef. Fish and shrimp are preferred to meat and poultry. The amount of poultry consumed is satisfied from within the country. No pork is eaten by Muslims, but the Chinese minority eats a great deal of pork, which is imported from Singapore and elsewhere. The need for fruits and vegetables cannot be fully met from within Brunei, and the

popularity of apples and other temperate-climate fruits demands that they be imported. In fact, about 90 percent of all food is imported. The staple food is rice and, although rice is the main crop in Brunei, the Bruneians import much of their rice—about 20,000 tons (18,144,000 kilograms) a year—from Thailand.

Among the other key industries in Brunei are logging and fishing. The fishing industry shows promise in several ways. Trawlers (specialized fishing boats that carry nets) have been introduced and have greatly increased the catches of ocean fish. Also being promoted are farms where giant prawns (shrimp) or freshwater fish are raised for Brunei's dinner tables and for restaurants. The ocean catches now total about 2,000 metric tons each year.

Using another natural resource, the country's 27 sawmills produce an average of 65 metric tons of high-quality timber each year. Brunei restricts the export of wood to sawed timber; uncut logs cannot be exported. Active seeding and other conservation programs ensure that lumber will remain a source of income in the future.

Since Brunei imports so many products, they have a trading relationship with many countries. The ones that bring the most products into Brunei are Singapore, then Japan, the United States, Great Britain, and Malaysia. Foreign goods consumed by the people of Brunei include clothing and electrical products from Singapore; cars, gasoline-powered and electrical appliances, and other products from Japan; chemicals, machinery, and aircraft from the United States; various goods from Great Britain; and food and clothing from Malaysia.

Opposite page: Shrimp farming is a growing business.

Live poultry (left) and fresh produce (right) can be purchased at local markets.

CONSUMER HEAVEN

Private enterprise thrives in the country, with shops selling everything from fruit to motorcycles to blue jeans to boom boxes. The traditional *tamu*, "open market," usually held once a week in a town of any size, features flowers, foods, crafts, reading materials, T-shirts, musical cassettes, and more. Besides providing income for an already well-to-do people, the tamu is a popular place to socialize.

There are nine banks with forty-one branch banks and several chambers of commerce. These organizations promote local

Ginger, citrus fruits, and turtle eggs are some of the items for sale at this market.

business and help Bruneian and foreign businessmen meet. The government has encouraged foreign investment, as long as all foreign-backed business ventures include the participation of Bruneians.

Most of the foreigners who come to the country are not tourists; they are connected in some way to the oil business. The Brunei tourist industry is geared for local tourism. The country has a few nice hotels and wide stretches of beach, but there is little need for the money international tourists bring. Equally important, keeping foreign visitors to a reasonable number helps preserve Brunei customs and traditions.

The magnificent Omar Ali Saifuddin Mosque, completed in 1958, is made of Italian marble and has gold leaf on the dome. An interior court of the mosque is shown below.

Chapter 5

THE IMPORTANCE

OF ISLAM

"Is religion an important part of your life?" That question was asked of a mid-level Muslim political official.

"No," said the official, "it *is* my life."

The official's answer gives an accurate picture of the role Islam plays in the day-to-day conduct of government, business, and personal life in Brunei. Islam is the official religion, but it is much more, affecting even those who follow Buddhism, Christianity, a tribal religion, or no religion at all. To understand Brunei, it is necessary to learn about Islam.

FOLLOWING MUHAMMAD

There are 600 million Muslims, followers of the Islamic religion, worldwide. About 150,000 of them are the people of Malay descent who are Bruneians. They trace their religion back through history to Arabia in the seventh century A.D. A prophet named Muhammad called in A.D. 622 for commitment to the one God, whom he called Allah.

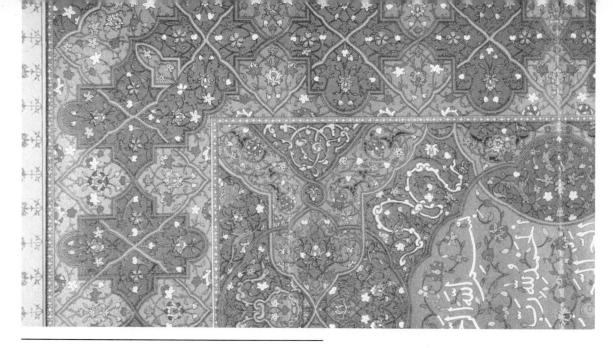

A part of the Koran: the revered Holy Book of Brunei

Communities led by men who believed in this single God—Allah—flourished, spreading across the Middle East in its first one hundred years. They taught from the *Koran*, a book that contains sacred writings of Allah (God), as given to the prophet Muhammad. Believers state that the Koran is the word of God, put into Muhammad's heart by the angel Gabriel.

During the one thousand years that followed Muhammad's death, Islam continued to grow outward in all directions. Arab traders sailed to India and met many residents who eagerly accepted the religion. These people in turn traded with what is now Southeast Asia and Indonesia, converting others to the faith that originated in the Arabian desert.

By the time the British arrived in the nineteenth century, Malays and Indonesians all over Borneo looked to leaders such as the sultan of Brunei to protect and advance the religion of Islam. In fact, a sultan in this part of the world was as much a religious leader as a ruler. Religion and politics have always been inseparable in Brunei.

Male worshipers leaving Omar Ali Saifuddin Mosque, which boasts a 177-foot (54-meter) minaret

CIVIL LAW, RELIGIOUS LAW

Wisely, the British did not attempt to interfere with religious practice. Separate courts, which made sure religious law was followed, were set up and run by Bruneian Islamic judges. No wonder Brunei residents today continue to look with great friendship on the British, who introduced Western political ideas without trying to alter centuries of deeply held beliefs.

How does a person become a Muslim? He or she can begin the Muslim experience by stating the desire to do so. However, most Bruneians are born into the religion. To be considered a Muslim, a person must follow the Five Pillars of Faith.

1. *The Profession of Faith:* Every Muslim must accept the supremacy of God and that Muhammad is his prophet.
2. *Prayer:* A believer must pray five times daily. He or she must bow in the direction of Mecca, Muhammad's birthplace in Saudi Arabia, during prayers.
3. *The Zakat and Fitrah* (religious tax and alms for the poor): The tax must be paid annually on most possessions. Muslims must give alms to the poor.
4. *Fasting:* Muslims must not eat or drink between sunrise and sunset for one entire month each year. This holy month is called *Ramadan.* Even the Muslim restaurants are closed during the day at this time.
5. *The Hajj* (pilgrimage): Every Muslim is expected to make a religious trip to the holy city of Mecca once in his or her lifetime, if possible. The pilgrimage to Mecca is expensive. Several government-backed sources will lend Muslims money for the trip without charging interest.

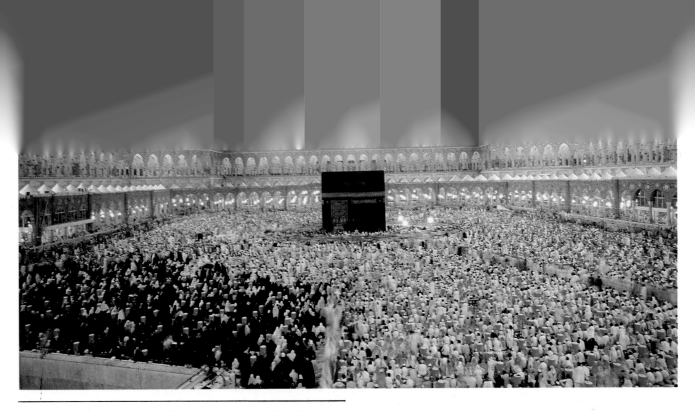

Muslim pilgrims in Mecca, Saudi Arabia

Brunei residents are members of the Sunni Muslim sect. It is one of two main divisions in Islam and traces its beliefs back to the political division that followed the death of the prophet Muhammad. Sunnis see themselves as being the orthodox branch of Islam. One of the reasons Islam has spread across the globe is because it is strong and simple, with just a few rules that can be neither bent nor broken.

Voices from loudspeakers boom across the country five times a day, calling Muslims to prayer. Muslims may pray at home, in the mosque, or wherever they are. In Brunei, women seldom go to the mosque for sunset prayers each day or for prayers on special holy days. But Brunei men all have the religious duty to attend the mosque for the special noon prayers on Friday. And for those who are Muslim, but who choose not to obey the rules, there are religious police officers.

RELIGIOUS POLICE

The religious policemen stroll about Bandar Seri Begawan, much as a policeman might walk a beat. If they see a Muslim drinking an alcoholic beverage, for example, they will dash into the bar or restaurant, grab the person and haul him away from the half-consumed drink. Another rule is *khalwat*. This means "close proximity" and involves unmarried males and females. If the religious lawmen see two unmarried Muslims alone together, the pair will be warned that they should think about their morality, that they should not be alone together.

Non-Muslims visiting or living in Brunei can consume alcohol freely, but Muslims are expected to behave in a more approved way. Some Bruneian Muslims carry notes from their doctors stating that alcoholic beverages must be consumed for medical purposes. Some Muslims break the fast of Ramadan because of physical or medical problems. The religious police carefully watch for people who are not fasting when they should be, and when they find them, they take them before the religious court.

One of the Five Pillars of Islam is giving alms to the poor. This idea is very important to Muslims. It fits Brunei perfectly; the sultan uses the vast amounts of money from oil production to see to it that everyone in his little kingdom can survive. The Koran warns that hoarding wealth while there are poor people will result in terrible punishment.

Evidence of Islam is everywhere in Brunei today. In addition to the voice of the *muezzin*, the person who calls fellow Muslims to prayer, the architecture shows heavy influence from the Middle East. Buildings are adorned with endless, intricate designs; domes; and towers called *minarets*.

The entrance to the Omar Ali Saifuddin Mosque

Illegally parked! A policewoman tickets a parked car.

ISLAM AND SOCIETY

A Muslim who follows his faith finds a great deal of comfort in the Koran. This book can provide answers to questions about morality, personal behavior, a Muslim's relationship with God, and more. However, there are modern situations where the Koran and society clash. One of these is the position of women.

The Koran says that women must be subordinate to men. Muslim women in Brunei are very fortunate. Girls receive the same type of education as boys do, and many women have become university graduates, either in Brunei or overseas. Some Brunei women do not work outside the home, and others do traditional work such as running stores or selling things in the market. Women are active in the economy, and many women hold important jobs. It is true, however, that almost all the very highest positions are held by men.

A Chinese temple

OTHER RELIGIONS

Most Indian residents are Muslims, but a few follow India's traditional religion, Hinduism. Some Chinese Bruneians are Christian. Most persons of Chinese descent are Buddhists, with an emphasis on ancestor worship. Buddhism, which began twenty-five hundred years ago in India, teaches that people should strive for *nirvana,* "salvation." This salvation comes by living virtuously and results in a painless, eternal existence.

Some Chinese mix ancestor worship with Buddhism, which is most often seen in Brunei in the tiny, red-and-gold altars in homes and shops. Homeowners and shopkeepers fill these altars with offerings of fruit and incense to the Buddha or to Chinese deities. One of Bandar Seri Begawan's nicest nongovernment buildings is a multicolored Chinese temple.

The people of Brunei, like people elsewhere in the modern world, have mixed feelings about religion. Some are very devout, others are not. Chinese Buddhism, Christianity, Islam, and other religions all have different holidays at different times of the year. In Brunei religion is more than just beliefs; religion is also a statement about who one is. Brunei Malays appreciate the modern world and enjoy its gadgets and conveniences; however, they also say that it is important to keep a balance—to observe traditions and Islam—and they do.

His majesty, Sultan Hassanal Bolkiah, summed up his view of Brunei as an Islamic state in his keynote speech to the United Nations in 1984:

"We wish to be left alone, and free from foreign intervention. We want to build our country and give our people an even better life. We wish to see the realization of our aims for accelerated economic growth, social progress, and cultural development.

"We are determined to continue to modernize our country while keeping faith with the principles of our ancient faith, Islam. We are confident of the possibilities of success."

Chapter 6

GOVERNMENT
UNDER A SULTAN

Residents of Brunei Darussalam refer to their leader simply as the sultan. That's because his names and titles take up a lot of room. Officially, he is known as His Majesty Paduka Seri Baginda Sultan Haji Hassanal Bolkiah Mu'izzaddin Waddaulah, D.K.M.B., D.K., P.S.S.U.B., D.P.K.G., D.P.K.T., P.S.P.N.B., P.S.N.B., P.S.L.J., S.P.M.B., P.A.N.B., G.C.M.G., D.M.N., D.K. (Kelantan), D.K. (Johor), D.K. (Negeri Sembilan), Collar of the Supreme Order of the Chrysanthemum, Grand Order of Mugunghwa, D.K. (Pahang), Bintang Republik Indonesia Adipurna, Collar of the Nile, The Order of Al-Hussein bin Ali, The Civil Order of Oman, D.K. (Selangor), D.K. (Perlis), D.K. (Perak), The Ancient Order of Sikatuna Rank of Rajah, Al Khalifia, Ouissam El Mohammdi Grand Collier, The Most Auspicious Order of the Rajamitrabhorn, D.U.B.S. (Sarawak), P.G.A.T., Sultan and Yang Di-Pertuan Brunei Darussalam. It's all right to refer to him as Sultan Hassanal Bolkiah.

A BIG SPENDER

The sultan receives an annual allowance. Like many other monarchs the sultan has foreign investments. These foreign properties include a home in California and a department store and hotel in London.

Although the sultan is not really a flashy person, tales of his spending are amazing. Once, on a visit to the Middle East, Sultan Hassanal Bolkiah saw a Boeing 727 jet plane he liked. Told that it was for sale for $18 million, he pulled out his personal checkbook and wrote a check on the spot for the entire amount. His aircraft include two helicopters, three Boeing 727s, and one smaller passenger jet.

In 1984, when Brunei joined the United Nations, the sultan gave the city of New York $550,000 for its elderly, ill, and homeless. He recently created a $50,000 annual award for the person whose writing reflects the style of the late American author, Ernest Hemingway. Obviously, he is a very generous person.

One of the reasons the sultan spends a lot of money is linked to the belief that the health and well-being of the monarch equals the health and well-being of the country. So although it seems strange to people in democracies to see a king or sultan spend large amounts of money for the people of the country, it means things are going well with the nation.

THE SULTAN

His majesty is the eldest son of the twenty-ninth sultan in a line that dates back more than five hundred years. He was born in 1946 and was installed as crown prince (successor to the sultan)

*Prince Charles of Great Britain and Sultan Hassanal Bolkiah at
the National Day celebration in 1984 (left) and the sultan's father,
Sultan Omar Ali Saifuddin, in 1964 (right)*

in 1961. He received his early education in Brunei and Malaysia
before being sent to England. Already fluent in English when he
arrived in Britain in 1966, His Highness Hassanal Bolkiah was
enrolled in the Royal Military Academy at Sandhurst. His father,
Sultan Omar Ali Saifuddin, decided in October 1967 to turn over
the reins of the government to his son, who became Brunei's
twenty-ninth ruler. The current sultan guided the small, oil-rich
nation to complete independence from Britain in 1984.

In addition to being the head of state, Sultan Hassanal Bolkiah
serves as prime minister and as defense minister. He enjoys the
military (he was promoted to the rank of captain while in military
school) and he is very interested in defense matters. As a matter of
fact, the sultan's formal portrait shows him wearing a gold and
white military uniform bedecked with numerous medals.

Along with the uniform go a huge sword and a yellow
umbrella. The umbrella is carried by an attendant when the sultan

is outdoors on certain formal occasions. The yellow umbrella is the symbol of his position as rajah or king. The sultan looks just as dignified in custom-tailored suits from London, which he wears when meeting with dignitaries such as the British prime minister or the president of Japan.

THE SULTAN AS PRIME MINISTER

As Brunei's prime minister, Sultan Hassanal Bolkiah is in charge of foreign policy, the police, customs officials, public service (government workers), the detention center (jail), the anticorruption bureau, the petroleum department, government finances, and broadcasting and information. As minister of defense, he is in charge of all of the armed forces.

Defense forces include a brigade of men with all sorts of weapons, an air wing, and several missile-armed ships. Sultan Hassanal Bolkiah also leads the Gurkha Reserve Unit, a group of fierce Nepalese and Indian men whose ability as soldiers is legendary. The sultan is responsible for the day-to-day administration of the government also. With his many titles and vast wealth, it's hardly an exaggeration to say that the sultan *is* Brunei.

The sultan is advised by a Cabinet made up of ten men. Two members of the Cabinet are the sultan's brothers, Prince Muda Mohamed Bolkiah and Prince Muda Jefri Bolkiah. Prince Mohamed is minister for foreign affairs, while Prince Jefri is the finance minister. The sultan receives advice from several councils: religious, privy (senior advisors), succession, legislative, and ministerial.

Each year on the sultan's birthday, July 15, the capital city of

Opposite page: Headquarters of the Brunei Department of Religious Affairs

Bandar Seri Begawan is festive with decorations, lights, signs, and parades. Public and private buildings are covered with flashing bulbs and signs wishing the ruler long life. Ornate arches, high over city streets, are created just for the occasion. As a sign of his mercy, Sultan Hassanal Bolkiah usually sets free a few prison inmates to cap off the birthday celebration. The festivities sometimes last for ten days.

THE LEGAL SYSTEM

The legal system is based on English common law. Civil laws are created by the legislature. The Supreme Court is appointed by the sultan and consists of a high court and a court of appeals. Brunei currently uses the judicial committee of the Privy Council in London as the final court of appeal. The religious courts are separate courts that make decisions in religious matters. Religious courts handle all matters of marriage and divorce for Muslims. The religious courts fine Muslims who drink alcohol or who eat in public during the daytime in the fasting month.

DRUGS AND THE GOVERNMENT

Illegal drugs are a worldwide problem. In Brunei there are many people with time on their hands who are potential drug abusers. Consequently, Sultan Hassanal Bolkiah has taken a personal interest in erasing drug abuse in his country. Schoolchildren and military personnel are tested randomly and there is a government-sponsored drug rehabilitation center in the nation's capital.

Information collected so far shows that the typical drug abuser in Brunei is a male between the ages of twenty and thirty and tends to be from the less wealthy parts of society. The most commonly abused drugs are heroin and marijuana, smuggled in from Southeast Asia. Addicts who turn themselves in are treated for six months.

ABSOLUTE POWER

The sultan does not allow any of his subjects to criticize his monarchy or introduce any other form of government to the small nation. He has urged Bruneians to concentrate "on economic matters and the building of a healthy and highly disciplined society free of social scourges [problems]."

While most of his countrymen are happy, dissenters are of two different types: some want a more strict Muslim state while others want democracy.

Western journalists recently came under fire by the Bruneian government. The media people were accused of printing "coffee-shop gossip" by a member of the prime minister's office. The official said Westerners "can never give a true picture of events in Brunei," and he warned local journalists not to use the same tactics. This kind of warning is how the government controls the media: news people are careful about how they report things that are controversial, antigovernment, or tend to make anyone important look foolish.

The sultan probably will continue to rule and his son will follow after him, in turn. His majesty has stated clearly his view of government: "We will uphold the principle that each country has the inalienable right to establish its own form of government . . ."

Brunei International Airport opened in 1974.

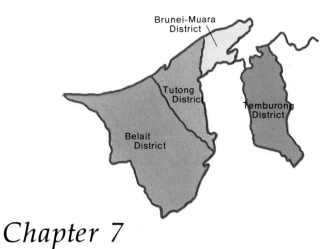

Chapter 7

A VISIT TO BRUNEI

A visit to Brunei begins as a commercial airline jet glides onto a runway at the Brunei International Airport, near the town of Berakas. The airport is extremely modern. One runway is 2.5 miles (4.8 kilometers) long so that even the very biggest planes can land with ease. The terminal is used by 400,000 passengers a year and has six gates.

Airlines flying to Brunei include Royal Brunei Airlines, Qantas, Cathay Pacific, British Airways, Singapore Airlines, Malaysian Air System, and Philippine Airlines. From here, a passenger can fly directly to Australia, Hong Kong, Malaysia, the Philippines, Singapore, or Taiwan. It's also possible to take an airline named Merpati Nusantara to places such as Balikpapan, Indonesia.

Bandar Seri Begawan is a fifteen-minute taxi ride from the airport. Unlike many other roads in Southeast Asia, this highway is wide and smooth with fresh pavement. Snazzy streetlights on shiny aluminum poles and carefully tended gardens hint that the

Above: Bandar Seri Begawan is on the Brunei River.
Below: People who live in the water village arrive at a landing stage
for a day's work in the capital.

The Churchill Memorial Museum

visitor is in a very up-to-date place. People from Canada, Great Britain, Malaysia, Singapore, and other British Commonwealth countries need no visa, but Mexicans and Americans, for example, must obtain a Brunei visa (an entry-permit stamp for their passport) before they land at the airport.

It's a good idea for a visitor to have plenty of money and a return airline ticket because the cost of living is high.

BANDAR SERI BEGAWAN

Gold minarets and ultramodern office buildings mix with Chinese shop houses and houses built on stilts over river water in this fascinating capital. Shops, restaurants, and coffee houses, most of them air conditioned, are packed all day long. The hot, humid air is clear at sunup, but it soon takes on a light odor of fish, diesel fuel, auto exhausts, blossoms, incense, tobacco, and spicy food. Yet everything is neat and clean.

The Bruneians wear a mixture of Eastern, Middle Eastern, and Western clothing.

People on the street wear baggy Chinese trousers, modern business suits, jeans and casual T-shirts, fashionable skirts and dresses, or shirts and *sarongs*—long strips of cloth that are wrapped around the body to form skirts—and occasionally Middle Eastern men's *kaftans* (robes). Cassettes of Malaysian and American rock singers blend with competing cassettes of Middle Eastern music. Signs and posters offer information about the shops and prices in three languages and three scripts: Malay, Chinese, and English.

The capital is nine miles (fourteen kilometers) from the mouth of the Brunei River and the sea. It has an area of about ten square miles (twenty-six square kilometers). Approximately fifty-seven thousand people live here, making it the largest city in the most populous of the country's four districts.

Homes and shops of Kampung Ayer are built on wooden or concrete posts and pilings.

THE WATER VILLAGE

About half of the city's population—thirty thousand—live in the fascinating *Kampung Ayer,* which means "water village." This village, built on wooden poles and stilts that keep the homes and shops about six feet (two meters) above the river, has been in existence for centuries. It was first described in 1521 by Antonio Pigafetta, a member of Ferdinand Magellan's round-the-world voyage.

At that time, garbage and sewage fell between cracks or were dumped off porches into the river. Conditions were unsanitary and unsafe, but Brunei has changed all that. At first, the British in the early part of the twentieth century, and later, the sultan, tried to lure people away from their watery homes on stilts by offering

Even a mosque is on pilings in Kampung Ayer.

them newly built homes on solid ground. The Kampung Ayer
residents politely declined.

So the sultan's officials provided telephones, electricity, clean
drinking water, clinics, and schools—all perched a few feet above
the muddy river. Cottage industries flourish in the huge village;
they include weaving, working with silver and brass, and many
kinds of crafts. Most adults who live here work for the
government. Their shiny new cars await them in Kampung Ayer's
huge parking lot nearby.

Boats in several sizes serve the water village. There are daily
school boats that whisk kids to classes. There are fishing boats that
haul nets out and fish in. And there are narrow, lightning-quick
boats with high-powered outboard motors to take residents from

Boats speed along one of the wide waterways in Kampung Ayer.

their homes to their cars and back. Malays have for centuries been skilled at building watertight boats of wood in all sizes—from these pencil-shaped speedsters to large, oceangoing sailboats. In fact, wealthy Europeans and others sometimes hire Malays to custom build craft for them.

Daring boat owners from the village race around and between the stilts and the newer and larger wood—and even concrete—supports. There are several wide waterways through the village, but many more where room for two boats side-by-side barely exists. Somehow, boating accidents are rare, and the village's many children are rarely injured when they swim in this churning highway. Children in Kampung Ayer learn to swim before they walk.

*Omar Ali Saifuddin Mosque is on a man-made lagoon
that is partly surrounded by the water village.*

The huge concrete boat, on which national Koran-reading competitions are held, resembles a sixteenth-century royal barge.

A STRIKING MOSQUE

Next to the water village is the magnificent Omar Ali Saifuddin Mosque. One of the most impressive buildings in all of Asia, the mosque was completed in 1958 at a cost of more than $5 million. It is a combination of Italian marble, gold mosaic, and stained glass. The interior is simple, tasteful, and quiet, while the shimmering exterior is made even more attractive by gardens and reflecting pools.

Its minaret, the tower from which Muslims are called to prayer, is 175 feet (54 meters) high and has an elevator inside. Linked to the mosque and built in the middle of a lagoon is a huge concrete boat that resembles a sixteenth-century royal barge. Contests for children to see who is best at reading the Koran are held on the boat.

There are other huge buildings in this small capital city. They include: the *Lapau*, "royal ceremonial hall." This is part of a

A complex of government buildings (above) includes the palace, Parliament House, and Royal Ceremonial Hall. A statue of Winston Churchill (below) stands in front of the museum dedicated to him.

sprawling complex that combines Malay and European architecture. The throne here was the site of the present sultan's 1968 coronation.

The *Dewan Majlis*, "Parliament House," is part of the Lapau complex. This building is surrounded by beautiful plants and fountains.

There are three museums, with the Brunei Museum the largest and most important. In it are hundreds of items representing the culture and history of the country. There is a Winston Churchill Museum and a museum of Malay technology. Brunei has many vibrant artists. There is a statue of Sir Winston Churchill in front of the Churchill Museum.

Hassanal Bolkiah Aquarium shares a large, crescent-shaped building with the Churchill Museum, while the ten-story arts and handicrafts center features numerous crafts demonstrations. Other impressive, newer buildings house the Supreme Court and the legal department.

The government buildings are filled with people who are bureaucrats—government workers. They fill out forms, write reports and follow procedures. There are many procedures to follow, since the sultan is a ruler who values order. These workers are well educated, frequently speak excellent English, and serve on numerous committees. Offices are sometimes overwhelmed with paperwork, but no one is frantic to finish what he or she is doing.

As nice as these and other structures are, they cannot compare to the sultan's huge *Istana*, "palace." Visible from many points in Bandar Seri Begawan, the Istana Nurul Iman is lighted at night and sits on a slight rise across the river from the city. The building alone covers many acres and is the size of a small town. In addition to the sultan's palace, it houses several government

The entrance to the sultan's palace

offices. In this way, it is like the White House in Washington, D.C., with rooms for the president and his family, but many more rooms for government offices and state functions. The palace rooms are not open to the public, except on special occasions, but with gold and marble everywhere, they are very elegant.

Just about the time that a visitor thinks Bandar Seri Begawan is so quiet it's dull, something exciting will happen. From out of nowhere come the sounds of sirens and the roar of powerful motorcycles. A dozen or more uniformed police roar into the main shopping area, blocking sidestreets and clearing a main route of all traffic.

Once the street is empty, a pearl-white, two-seater Mercedes-Benz blasts into view. It dives around a sharp turn, zooms past

The park in front of the Parliament House

staring citizens, and disappears. Who was it, the sultan? One of his sons? A family member? Since the glass in the car is deeply tinted, there is no way to tell. The police depart noisily, as quickly as they came. Life returns to its normal, pleasant pace.

Not everything in the capital is a building. The sports and exhibition fields are a deep green year round and are surrounded with flowering bushes. On the edge of town is a pleasant little park. A stream with a waterfall runs through the greenery, and to escape the heat children cavort in a swimming hole beneath the falls. Unfortunately, Bruneians who come here don't always pick up after themselves—there is litter along roads and footpaths. Yet it's quiet and peaceful.

A street (left) and a covered sidewalk market (right) in Kuala Belait

BRUNEI'S OTHER TOWNS

There are only a few other large towns in the country. They are Muara, Pekan Tutong, Seria, and Kuala Belait. Seria is the most important economically. Here, forty miles (sixty-four kilometers) southwest of the capital, is the site of the world's largest liquefied natural gas plant. Since Seria also is the gateway to the offshore oil business, this is where one is most apt to hear Australian or American accents. The refinery at Seria is a maze of shiny piping, with a real high-tech appearance. Away from the sea, some tribal villages can be visited inland.

Muara, fifteen miles (twenty-four kilometers) to the northeast from the capital on a large peninsula, is the main port of entry for ocean shipping. The modern harbor, with its large warehouse and small boats scurrying about, takes care of most ocean traffic, though there are smaller ocean ports at Bandar Seri Begawan and

An Iban longhouse

at Kuala Belait. The beaches near Muara are nice, and watching expensive yachts pull into anchor is a relaxing way to spend some time.

At the other extreme, simple living can still be found by the adventurous. Upriver in Temburong live Muruts and Ibans. Muruts are the native tribal people and Ibans are recent immigrants who arrived in Brunei during the last one hundred years. These tribes were led by headhunting warriors in the past. Today, some of the Ibans live in longhouses—buildings with sometimes dozens of rooms, each room sheltering a family—on

Iban carefully maneuvering their canoes over rocks

Brunei riverbanks. Wise in the ways of the forest, the Muruts and Ibans grow rice, some root crops and vegetables, and they hunt and fish. In the past few years, fewer men can be found living in the villages. That is because there is a labor shortage in Brunei and adult men can earn good money working away from their forest homes.

A VILLAGE UNDER ONE ROOF

Visiting a longhouse is quite an education. The longhouses nearer the capital city of Bandar Seri Begawan have many conveniences—outboard motors, chain saws, sewing machines, wood or natural gas cookstoves, and more. Much of this equipment is either people powered or run on gasoline or diesel fuel because electricity has just come to the area. Pigs, goats, dogs, and cats live beneath the house and fight over food scraps that are

Longhouses bustle with the various activities of daily life.

Above: An Iban with tattoos on his back and arms.
Left: Rice is pounded to remove the husk and
then dropped through a hole in the trough
to be collected.

pushed between the cracks onto the ground. Bathroom facilities
are downstream and bathing facilities upstream.

Ancient Chinese porcelain and ceramic bowls, worth hundreds
of dollars to antique dealers worldwide, are necessities here and
are used every day. Decorations in the homes consist of old
calendars or pages torn from magazines. Some very young
children wear little or no clothing and men frequently wear only
shorts and T-shirts. People are either barefoot or wear tennis
shoes.

Adults hunt, work in the fields, and prepare food, while older
children look after the younger children. Folk medicine and
traditional beliefs are still important parts of life, but there also is
free Western medical care for all Bruneians.

An Iban carrying a child on his back.

FOREIGN RESIDENTS

Foreign residents, many living in or near Seria, form another large group. These are the foreigners who work on the oil rigs owned jointly by the Shell Oil Company and the government of Brunei. Many of these geologists, engineers, and skilled laborers come to Brunei for a few years with their families, work hard and save money, and then return to their own countries.

Other foreigners live in the capital. These people, who live in the country with their families, are part of the international diplomatic and business community. They take advantage of good housing, pleasant beaches and parks, modern schools, and the experience a foreign way of life brings.

A colorfully painted house of Kampung Ayer

Chapter 8

THE CULTURE OF BRUNEI

English-speaking people first learned about life in this part of the world from Europeans. Joseph Conrad, a Pole who migrated to England after seeing the world for twenty years as a sailor, wrote dramatic short stories and novels of the South Seas in English—such as *Lord Jim*. His readers followed heroes who tried to make big decisions in a tropical setting where nature had no concern about the outcome. Because the novels were often tragic, readers mistakenly assumed anywhere tropical was dangerous. The settings were Borneo and other islands in the area. Conrad made several voyages around Borneo in 1887.

Another writer who used this tropical setting was W. Somerset Maugham, an Englishman. This medical doctor's twentieth-century novels, plays, and short stories are set in the South Seas and depict a feeling of tension that a tropical climate could create. Maugham liked to portray Europeans whose emotions get the best of them in foreign surroundings.

Both writers gave readers the idea that tragedy was a common occurrence in faraway places such as Brunei. That is unfair to

91

Bruneians in more ways than one. First, living in Brunei has never been any more dangerous than anywhere else. In fact, driving on a Western freeway is probably more of a threat than is zipping down the Brunei River in a speedy outboard. Second, writers like Conrad and Maugham took advantage of the fact that there was no strong literary tradition in the part of the world where they set many of their stories. As we will see, a rich heritage does not have to be based on novels and short stories.

VERBAL ENTERTAINMENT

For hundreds of years before Europeans came, Borneo residents passed along their history through stories and legends. Some of these tales were introduced by Hindus from India. They taught island people their religion by reciting epic stories from a book called the *Ramayana*. This tells of a god and his efforts to rescue his wife, who has been captured by an evil person. The Muruts too have an epic tradition. The storyteller recites stories about heroes and warriors, fights with pirates, and dugout races. Using many voices for the characters, the storyteller weaves a magic tapestry about the past. What a wonderful way to pass the time on a soft, tropical night.

CLEVER WAYS WITH CLOTH

Cloth weaving is among Brunei's oldest cottage industries. For centuries girls and women have worked on wooden looms in the home to produce material of incredible beauty. The most famous product is *jong sarat*, which results from mixing cloth threads among threads of silver and gold. Jong sarat is seen in all royal

Cloth weaving is an ancient and prized form of art.

ceremonies, in weddings, as wall hangings in wealthy homes, and now as gifts and souvenirs. The patterns are amazingly complex. Some are geometric and abstract designs like those that adorn ceilings in an Islamic mosque; others are floral patterned.

METALWARE

Hammers no bigger than spoons are used to work on metal, especially silver. This is a cottage industry, too. It is done with a skill that has been handed down from parent to child for

A silversmith tapping in a design

centuries. Nowadays, many people can own silverware that features tiny, complicated designs done by hand on each piece.

Bronze and brass items are created, too. This craft is practiced in small shops but can be seen everyday in the new, ten-story Arts and Handicrafts Center on the banks of the Brunei River in Bandar Seri Begawan.

BASKETRY

Yet another craft is weaving with leaves and strands of vegetation. Wonderful baskets, mats, hats, handbags, and more are made using nothing but a learned skill, bare hands, and immense patience. The woven leaf products are made of bamboo, screw-pine leaves, and other ready materials.

The Arts and Handicrafts Center was built to preserve the arts of cloth making, basketry, and metalwork. In a land with as many modern conveniences as Brunei, that may be the best way to maintain ancient skills.

Chapter 9

EVERYDAY LIFE

Brunei is a very young country in more ways than one. It became a completely independent country in 1984. But it is young, too, in the average age of the people. Almost half of the population is under the age of twenty, with 14 percent being of preschool age. The average age of Brunei's people should remain young for quite a while, since there is no need at the moment to limit family size or total population.

EDUCATION

With so many young residents, education should be difficult for the government to provide. But it isn't thanks once again to the huge amount of money brought in each year from oil and natural gas. Education is free to everyone in Brunei, from his or her first day of school to the limits of the student's ability. For citizens this is true whether the child attends a government or private school, at home or abroad.

The variety of schools in the country is amazing. There are one university, one teachers' college, one institute of technology, one

religious teachers' college, one college of nursing, five vocational-technical schools, 153 primary schools, 18 high schools, and 112 preschools.

More than forty-five thousand young people attend government-run schools, which are taught in Malay, English, or Arabic. There are also numerous adult education centers scattered across the country, aimed at teaching skills to those whose lives might have prevented them from getting an education earlier. Nongovernment schools number sixty-nine and include a training

Muslim girls going to school

school run by the Brunei Shell Oil Company, plus missionary and Chinese schools where the language used is either a Chinese dialect or English.

School attendance is mandatory for six years. All over the country, a visitor can easily spot children going to or coming home from school. That is because students wear simple uniforms—white shirts or blouses with dark blue or green shorts for the boys and skirts for the girls. Uniforms are required at most public and private elementary and secondary schools.

LANGUAGE

Malay is the first language of all Bruneians of Malay descent. It is an elegant language, spoken or understood (with some variation) from the southern Philippines westward, through Indonesia, and into Malaysia. Malay does not have the sing-song quality of Chinese and is therefore easier for English-speaking persons to learn to pronounce. English is the language of business and is taught in almost every school. The Chinese spoken in Brunei is usually Cantonese or a similar south China dialect. Other languages include Arabic and the tribal tongues, which are being replaced by Malay as the country becomes more developed.

SOCIAL SERVICES

No one needs to worry about paying a doctor bill in Brunei. Free medical care is provided in five hospitals, dozens of clinics and dispensaries, and a flying doctor service that treats people in remote areas. There are also numerous private clinics, often run by Chinese, throughout the country. The country's largest hospital is in Bandar Seri Begawan and has facilities the equal of anywhere in Asia. Between attentive health service and willingness to spend money for prevention, diseases such as malaria and childhood diseases are rare. Compared to other tropical countries Brunei has a high standard of health.

Pensions have been given to older people since 1955. These monthly checks are given to the elderly, people who are disabled, and any dependents they might have. Unlike most countries, none of the citizens have to pay their own share into the national pension fund.

Offices of Brunei Shell in Seria

The government and Brunei Shell are the country's two largest employers. Both provide their employees with housing. The government has gone one step further—landless Bruneians, whether employed by the government or not, can own a plot of land and a house at a fraction of the true cost. People living in these houses repay the government some money each month. Private builders also offer luxury homes and high-rise apartment living.

FOOD

Like all of Southeast Asia, rice is the backbone of the Brunei diet. People of Malay, Chinese, or tribal descent rely on rice to accompany whatever else they have with their meals. It is these additions to rice that make the diets of the ethnic groups different.

Above: Fresh fish for sale in a market
Left: A water buffalo pulls a canoe
through a rice field.

A Brunei meal cooked in the home is eaten with the right hand (the left hand is considered unclean). Spoons and forks are used to move food from a serving dish to a plate, but the bare hand then is used for actual eating. There are very specific rules for eating with one's hands. Since the food tends to be bite-sized, knives are unnecessary.

The menu can include fish, shrimp, chicken, water buffalo, or beef, vegetables cooked in spicy sauces, and, of course, all the rice anyone can eat. Tea, coffee, and fruit juice are popular drinks. Since Muslims are forbidden to drink alcoholic beverages and eat pork, neither is found in Muslim homes.

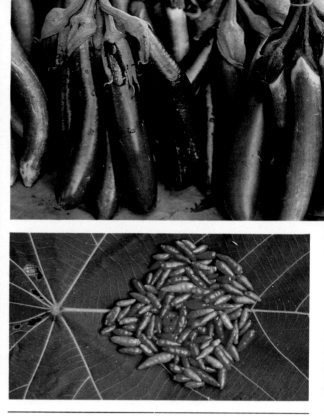

A variety of fruits and vegetables are eaten by Bruneians (left). Many dishes are completely vegetarian and may contain eggplants (top right), while others are spiced with hot red peppers (above).

People who trace their roots to mainland China are traditional pork eaters. So pork, chicken, fish, and shrimp are served in main-course dishes, atop the familiar mound of rice—or fried noodles. Some meals are quite filling without any meat. Vegetables are cooked with or without meat and flavored with tangy sauces that are not quite as spicy as the ethnic Malays' meal. Tea, fruit juice, soft drinks, and beer are popular mealtime drinks.

Chinese food and Malay *satay*, bits of charcoal-broiled chicken or beef on wooden skewers, are eaten out, as are Indian dishes that may be vegetarian and spiced with fiery peppers. Popular street-corner food includes small cakes, fried bananas, fresh fruit, fruit drinks, sugarcane juice, and soda.

When planting "dibbled" rice, seeds are dropped into prepared holes.

Tribespeople live on freshwater fish, wild game, root crops, and, of course, rice. Most of these people who grow rice raise it on dry land. It is called hill rice, in contrast to paddy or wet-rice production. Some of their foods, such as certain kinds of tasty, wild ferns, have found their way onto tables across the country.

In most Bruneian diets, meat is used for flavoring dishes more than it is the central part of a meal. A cook in a popular Chinese restaurant says that he can get more than a dozen different main dishes from a single chicken.

A polo match

SPORTS AND RECREATION

Brunei's most popular sport is soccer. There is a modern national stadium where Bruneians play each other and challenge teams from elsewhere in Southeast Asia. Because the country is so small, there simply aren't enough players of any one sport for a team to command international attention. The only other team sport of importance is polo, played by the sultan and his team. This group of experienced players and expensive horses plays throughout Southeast Asia. The sultan loves the game of polo, which was brought to Brunei by the English. Attached to the palace are stables for as many as two hundred polo ponies. Many of the stables are air conditioned since the ponies come from more temperate climates. Polo is not played by ordinary citizens, but some villagers are expert riders.

The golf course at Seria

The country's most commonly played game is *sepak takraw.* It can be played anywhere and it uses a hollow ball made of strips of lightweight rattan. The softball-sized ball is passed in a circle from one player to another, using feet, knees, heads, backsides — anything but hands. The object of the game, which is also played by two teams with a net, is to see how long the ball can be kept moving and off the ground.

Skilled players of this game are fascinating to watch, as are a couple of other sports: top spinning, an ancient Brunei art, and kite flying. Villagers see whose top can spin for the longest or whose kite can fly the highest. Such low-key activities make sense in a land that is always hot and humid. Other commonly played sports and games include Ping-Pong, badminton, and swimming.

The popularity of golf is increasing, despite the ever-present heat. There are two courses, one near the capital and another at Seria. Foreigners working in Brunei brave high temperatures to play golf. The national stadium, where soccer is played before crowds of as many as thirty-five thousand, also has facilities for track and field activities, weightlifting, swimming, and squash. Other forms of recreation include windsurfing, cycling, martial arts, and motor racing. Like most countries with a dependable electrical supply, video games can be found, usually in cities.

TRANSPORTATION

In other Southeast Asian countries, most people ride bicycles or small scooters or they hire a ride in a three-wheeled trishaw, pedaled by the driver. Not in Brunei, where the people seem to have gone from walking to owning shiny new cars. Automobiles, mostly from Japan, clog the streets of Bandar Seri Begawan. The roads are good, but with almost 100,000 cars in the country, space is at a premium. Rural roads are well paved, too, but there is no cross-country expressway.

The daily bus westward into Sarawak runs along the beach, weather permitting. Bruneians drive on the left side of the road like the British and Japanese.

This part of the world relies on ocean traffic to move goods to and from one country to another, but there is little or no passenger traffic. The majority of people never leave their country, while those who do leave can afford to fly. Top destinations are Singapore and Hong Kong for shopping sprees. There are a few oceangoing yachts, but they are not for general passenger use. Pirates are still a very real threat on Southeast Asian seas, particularly at the northern end of the island of Borneo. River

A plane from Royal Brunei Airlines

travel is still important for people. Citizens who travel by water here also usually run short distances—from their riverside villages to their parked cars.

Brunei's showcase form of transport is the government-owned airline. Formed in 1974, Royal Brunei Airlines has always been an all-jet fleet. It carries the yellow, white, and black color scheme of the country's flag and flies to Australia, Singapore, Hong Kong, and other destinations. Profitable since 1982, the line has several new Boeing 737 and 757 aircraft.

THE FUTURE

Sultan Hassanal Bolkiah says he will give his people a chance to help run the country when they really want it. At present, he believes, no one minds if the sultan, his family, and friends govern.

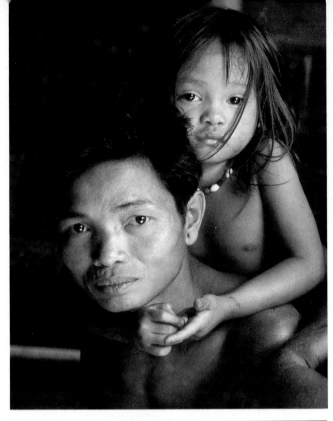

*The sultan of Brunei
cares for all his people.*

That is probably true. There is not likely to be any big move against the sultan as long as the rich supply of oil continues to be pumped and processed. Even though oil prices were low in the late 1980s, there was still plenty of money for Bruneians to share. But what happens around the year 2010 when the oil runs out? Maybe nothing. The sultan and his advisers have so much petroleum money to invest that, when the oil disappears, income will continue from other sources. It's possible that all of Brunei will one day live on interest and dividends from overseas loans and investments.

The sultan is a capable leader who cares for his people. For the foreseeable future, Brunei probably will continue to be a slow-and-easy place to live for every one of its citizens.

Bruneians sorting fish (above) and selling produce (opposite page)

Omar Ali Saifuddin Mosque is lighted at night.

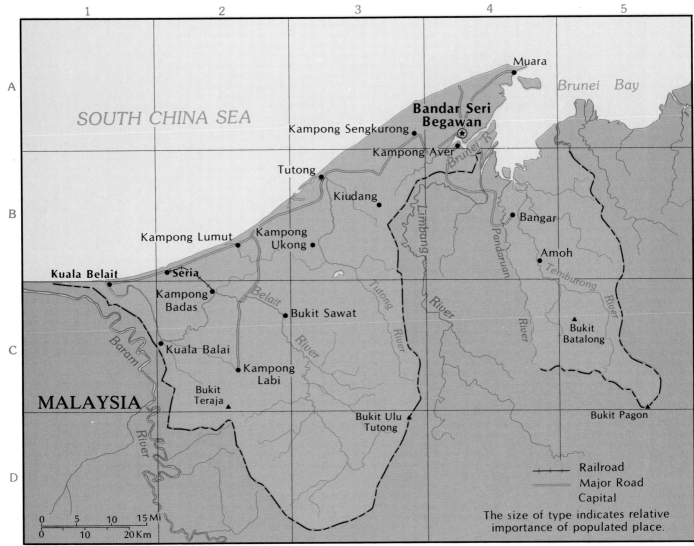

Map prepared by University of Kentucky Cartography Lab

MAP KEY

Amoh	B4	Kampong Labi	C2
Bandar Seri Begaqan	A4	Kampong Lumut	B2
Bangar	B4	Kampong Sengkurong	A3
Belait River	C2, C3	Kampong Ukong	B3
Brunei River	A4, B4	Kiudang	B3
Brunei Bay	A4, B4, A5	Kuala Balai	C2
Bukit Batalong	C5	Kuala Belait	C1
Bukit Pagon	C5	Muara	A4
Bukit Sawat	C2	Pandaruan River	B4, C4
Bukit Teraja	C2	Seria	B2
Bukit Ulu Tutong	D3	Temburong River	B4, B5, C5
Kampong Ayer	A4	Tutong	B3
Kampong Badas	C2	Tutong River	B3, C3

MINI-FACTS AT A GLANCE

GENERAL INFORMATION

Official Name: Negara Brunei Darussalam (State of Brunei, Abode of Peace)

Government: Brunei is an independent Islamic sultanate, with the capital at Bandar Seri Begawan. The sultan is the hereditary head of the government and state and enjoys absolute power. He is also the prime minister and defense minister. His Royal Highness Paduka Seri Pengiran Di-Gadong Sahibul Mal Pengiran Muda Haji Jefri Bolkiah (Prince Jefri Bolkiah) is minister of finance and Special Adviser to His Majesty the Sultan and Yang Berhormat Pehin Orang Kaya Laila Setia Bakti Di-Raja Dato Laila Utama Haji Awang Isa bin Pehin Datu Perdana Menteri Dato Laila Utama Haji Awang Ibrahim (Pahin Dato Haji Isa) is minister for home affairs. The sultan is advised by a Cabinet of eleven men. There is no legislature. The legal system is based on English Common Law and the criminal justice system is based on the Indian Penal Code. All Supreme Court judges are appointed by the sultan. The constitution provides for a Privy Council, a Council of Ministers, a Religious Council, and a Council of Succession. The 1959 constitution has been suspended since 1962, and the sultan has since ruled under a state of emergency. Brunei has no income tax.

Religion: Islam is the official religion followed by 67 percent of the population. Buddhism is followed by some 12 percent and Christianity by 9 percent. There are minorities following tribal religions. The sultan is head of the Islamic faith in Brunei and is the religious leader of his people. A Religious Council advises the sultan on all Islamic matters. Almost all Brunei Muslims adhere to the Sunni sect of Islam.

Ethnic composition: Almost 65 percent of Bruneians are Malays, 20 percent are Chinese, 8 percent are indigenous people (Muruts, Tutongs, Dusuns, Belaits, Penans, and Ibans), and 6 percent are foreign residents.

Language: The official language is Malay. However, all official documents are also published in English as it is the language of business. The Jawi alphabet is the same as Arabic with a few letters added from Persian. The Jawi script is used for writing both Malay and Indonesian.

National Flag: Yellow with two diagonal stripes of white and black running from the upper hoist to the outer edge. The state emblem, in red with yellow Arabic inscription, is superimposed in the center.

National emblem: The state crest was added to the flag in 1959. The bright red crest consists of a small flag and a royal umbrella. Just below these are wings of four feathers representing justice, tranquility, prosperity, and peace. One hand on either side represents government's pledge to promote wealth, peace, and prosperity. A large crescent representing Islam has the national motto inscribed, "Always render service by God's guidance." The scroll at the bottom reads, "Brunei Darussalam, Abode of Peace."

National Anthem: "Ya Allah lanjutkan usia" ("God bless His Highness with a long life")

Money: The Brunei dollar of 100 cents is valued at par with, and is interchangeable with, the Singapore dollar. In 1990 one Brunei dollar was equal to $.57 in U.S. currency.

Weights and Measures: Brunei uses the metric system.

Area and Population: The country is divided into four districts for administrative purposes.

Districts	Capitals	Area sq. mi.	sq km	Population 1989 estimates
Beloit	Kuala Belait.	1,052	2,724	58,100
Brunei and Muara	Bandar Seri Begawan.	220	571	153,200
Temburong	Bangar.	504	1,304	9,100
Tutong	Tutong.	450	1,166	28,600
Total		**2,226**	**5,765**	**249,000**

Population: 259,000 (1990 estimate). The density is 116.4 persons per sq. mi. (44.9 persons per sq km). Distribution is 64 percent urban, 36 percent rural. About 50 percent of the labor force work for the government.

Cities: (1981 estimates)

Bandar Seri Begawan	52,300 (1988 estimate)
Seria	23,511
Kuala Belait	19,281
Tutong	6,161

Nearly one-fifth of Brunei's population lives in the capital city. Seria with its offshore oil and natural gas fields is an economically important town. One of the world's largest liquefied natural gas plants is situated at Lumut. Muara is situated on the mouth of the Brunei River. With its deep-water facilities it is the main port of entry for ocean shipping.

GEOGRAPHY

Borders: North—South China Sea
South, East, and West—Malaysian state of Sarawak
Land boundary—236 mi. (381 km)
Coastline—100 mi. (161 km)

Land: Brunei occupies the northwestern coast of Borneo Island. Its eastern and western enclaves are separated by the Limbang River Valley of Sarawak state of Malaysia.

Highest point: Bukit Pagon at 6,040 ft. (1,841 m)

Lowest point: Sea level

Rivers: The major rivers are the Brunei, Belait, Tutong, Temburong, and Keduan. Rivers are the major avenues of communication with Brunei's interior. Much of the terrain in the river valleys is swampy.

Forests: More than one-half of Brunei is heavily forested. The forests are strictly protected by the government and timber export is restricted. Active seeding and conservation programs are in force year round. Mangrove swamps cover coastal regions. Orchids, hibiscus, and pitcher plants grow abundantly.

Wildlife: Tarsiers, proboscis monkeys, leaf monkeys, macaques, langurs, gibbons, bears, deer, wild cats, tropical birds and butterflies, shrews, turtles, and poisonous snakes reside in the forest areas. The rivers of Brunei and Brunei Bay are very rich in diverse fish species. The estuarine crocodile is listed under endangered species. Insects are abundant and sometimes harmful.

Climate: The climate is tropical with uniformly high temperatures, humidity, and rainfall. Average annual temperatures are 82° F. (28° C), and the relative humidity ranges between 67 percent and 91 percent. Rainfall is highly variable from place to place. November to March are usually the wetter months. The average rainfall is about 125 in. (317 cm) and it can reach more than 200 in. (508 cm) in the interior.

Greatest Distances: North to south—55 mi. (89 km)
East to west: 47 mi. (76 km)

ECONOMY AND INDUSTRY

Agriculture: Less than 2 percent of the land is under agriculture and permanent cultivation. Rice, coconut, fruits (guava, jackfruit, durian, pineapple, melons), yams, peppers, corn, beans, peas, cucumbers, and cassava are the major agricultural products. Brunei owns a beef-cattle ranch at Willeroo, northern Australia—the ranch is larger than the country of Brunei itself. This ranch provides for one-third of the total beef consumed in Brunei. McFarm, a Japanese assisted cattle-breeding station, was set up to reduce meat imports. Some 60 percent of fish consumption is provided by local fishermen. Fish catch largely consists of puthihan, haruan, shrimp, prawns, eels, grouper, and sharks. Fish hatcheries are in operation near Muara.

Mining: Oil and natural gas are the most important mineral resources. There are six offshore oil and gas fields near Seria. Crude oil is transported by pipelines to refineries. Brunei petroleum is expected to last till the year 2010. Oil production is controlled by Brunei Shell, the country's only oil company. Petroleum by-products are gasoline, jet fuel, diesel fuel, kerosene, asphalt, and wax. Brunei is the world's fourth-largest producer of liquid natural gas. The oil economy provides Brunei with the highest per capita income in Southeast Asia. More than 90 percent of Brunei's revenue comes from oil.

Manufacturing: Industries are largely limited to oil and natural gas and timber. Cottage industries are popular, and include weaving of *jong sarat* with silver, gold, and cotton thread, manufacturing of brass and silver wares, basket weaving, furniture, pottery and tile making, and boat building.

Transportation: There are only 12 mi. (20 km) of privately owned railroads. The total length of roads is about 1,200 mi. (1,930 km) out of which some 50 percent are paved. Autos are driven on the left side of the road. A main road connects Bandar Seri Begawan with Kuala Belait. The inland waterways cover about 130 mi. (209 km). The merchant marine consists of some 40 vessels. Bruneians are proud of their all-jet Royal Brunei Airlines that provides service to Great Britain, Germany, Australia, Singapore, Malaysia, Indonesia, the Philippines, Taiwan, Hong Kong, and Thailand. Brunei International Airport, near the capital, is the country's only large airport.

Communication: *Borneo Bulletin* (established 1953) is a daily English and Malay newspaper. *Palita Brunei* is a weekly Malay-language, government newspaper distributed free. *Brunei Darussalam Newsletter* is published monthly by the government. *Salam* is a free monthly Malay and English newsletter of Brunei Shell Petroleum Company. Radio Television Brunei broadcasts an all-color television service. There are about 50,000 TV sets, 75,000 radios, and some 35,000 telephones.

Trade: Oil and natural gas comprise more than 97 percent of Brunei's exports. Imports consists of clothing, electrical appliances, cars, chemicals, machinery, aircraft, and food items.

EVERYDAY LIFE

Holidays:

New Year's Day, January 1
Chinese New Year, variable (February 6 in 1989)

National Day, February 23
Me'raj, variable (March 5 in 1989)
First Day of Puasa (Ramadan), variable (April 7 in 1989)
Anniversary of the Revelation of the Koran, variable (April 23 in 1989)
Hari Raya Puasa, variable (May 6-7 in 1989)
Anniversary of the Royal Brunei Armed Forces, May 31
Hari Raya Haji, variable (July 13 in 1989)
Sultan's Birthday, July 15
First Day of Hijrah (Muslim New Year), variable (August 3 in 1989)
Maulud (The Prophet's Birthday; tenth day of the lunar new year), variable
    (October 12 in 1989)
Christmas Day, December 25
Chinese New Year and various Muslim holy days are movable holidays
    because they are based on lunar calendars.

Health: Brunei's health-care system is ranked as one of the finest in Asia.
Medical care is free for Bruneians. A flying doctor service and traveling
dispensaries treat people in remote areas. For medical care not available in Brunei,
citizens are sent abroad at the government's expense. Unlike many Southeast Asian
countries, cholera and childhood diseases are rare. Malaria has been completely
eradicated.

Education: Education is free at all levels. Educational opportunities are the same
for girls and boys and schooling is compulsory for six years. Schools operate a five-
day week with Fridays and Sundays off, and are closed for the month of Ramadan.
The language of instruction is Malay, English, or Arabic. Islamic religious
education is part of the curriculum both at government and private schools.
Technical education is offered by six vocational and technical schools. Teachers are
trained at the Institute of Education at Bandar Seri Begawan. The total student
population at the University of Brunei Darussalam numbers nearly 1,000. Many
students go abroad for higher studies at government expense. Almost 95 percent of
Bruenians can read.

Culture: The Brunei Museum displays items related to Brunei's culture and
history. Other cultural institutions are the Winston Churchill Memorial Museum,
the Museum of Malay Technology, the Sultan Hassanal Bolkiah Aquarium, the
Army Museum (1979), the National Stadium, the Arts and Handicrafts Training
Center, and the *Lapau* or the Royal Ceremonial Hall. Buildings noted for their
architecture are the Supreme Court Building, the colorful Chinese Temple, the

Omar Ali Saifuddin Mosque, and the *Dewan Majlis* or the Parliament House. The *Istana Nurul*, the sultan's 1,788-room palace on 50 ac. (20 ha) with two gold-leaf domes, is sometimes considered the largest private home on the earth. The National Library is in the capital city. There are public libraries in other main towns with mobile library services in remote areas.

Housing: An interesting feature in Brunei is the "Water Village," *Kampung Ayer*, with longhouses built on wooden poles and stilts about 6 ft. (2 m) above the Brunei River. Roughly one-half of the capital's population resides in the Water Village. Residents park their cars in the village parking lots and travel back and forth to their longhouse by small speedboats. Many people in the cities live in modern houses or apartment buildings.

Food: There is more emphasis on shrimp, fish, and poultry than on meat in Bruneian food. As Muslims do not eat pork, pork is largely imported from Singapore for the Chinese minority. The staple food is rice. Food is eaten with the right hand. The menu generally consists of rice, shrimp or fish, chicken, beef, and vegetables. Popular drinks are tea, coffee, and sugarcane and fruit juices; Muslims are forbidden to drink alcoholic beverages.

Sports and Recreation: The most popular sport is soccer, followed by Ping-Pong, badminton, golf, top spinning, and kite flying. Polo is played by the sultan and his team, but is not a game for ordinary citizens.

Social welfare: Starting in 1955, the government has been giving pensions to the elderly and disabled. Bruneians also receive wedding and burial allowances and subsidized food and housing.

IMPORTANT DATES

A.D. 500 — Chinese sailors visit Brunei

977 and 1082 — Brunei sends tribute to Chinese emperor

1371 — Islam reaches Brunei before this date

1521—Europeans arrive in Brunei

1600—Portuguese establish a trading factory and a Catholic mission at Brunei Town

1838—James Brooke arrives in Borneo

1839—Malays and Land Dayaks in Sarawak rebel against Brunei rule

1845—First American ship, the USS *Constitution*, visits Brunei

1847—The sultan enters into a treaty with Great Britain to enhance commercial relations and to suppress piracy

1850—United States-Brunei Friendship Treaty

1887—Joseph Conrad makes several voyages around Brunei; the sultan enters into a treaty with Great Britain to further commercial relations

1888—Brunei becomes a British protectorate

1906—Flag of Brunei created; first British resident arrives

1929—Oil is discovered off coast of Seria

1940—State motto of "Always render service by God's guidance" is added to the flag

1942-45—Brunei and northern coast of Borneo come under Japanese occupation during World War II

1950—Sultan Omar Ali Saifuddin ascends to the throne on the death of his brother

1955—Elderly and disabled Bruneians start getting government pensions

1957—British Malaya becomes self-governing Malaysia

1958 — Omar Ali Saifuddin Mosque is completed at the cost of $5,000,000

1959 — State crest is added to the flag; a new constitution is written declaring Brunei a self-governing state

1962 — Malaysian territory is threatened by Indonesia and Philippine troops; last legislative elections are held and the constitution is suspended; British troops are called in to put down rebellion

1963 — Brunei declines to become a Malaysian state; Sarawak and North Borneo become states of Malaysia

1965 — Natural gas deposits are found near Seria

1966 — A peace treaty between Indonesia and Malaysia is signed

1967 — On October 4, Sultan Omar Ali Saifuddin abdicates in favor of his eldest son

1968 — On August 1, coronation of Sultan Hassanal Bolkiah, the 29th ruler in succession, takes place

1970 — State capital is renamed Bandar Seri Begawan

1971 — A Gurkha battalion of British army is established

1973 — A liquefied natural gas plant opens at Lumut under the joint ownership between the Brunei government and Mitsubishi of Japan

1974 — Royal Brunei Airlines is formed; the Brunei International Airport opens

1975 — Color television is introduced

1976 — The Sinaut Agriculture Training Center opens; the Economic Development Board is set up by the government to assist new industries

1978 — Educational television is introduced

1979 — Sultan Muda Hassanal Bolkiah and British minister sign a new friendship treaty

1984 — On January 1, Brunei becomes the fully independent state of Brunei Darussalam and joins the United Nations; the Legislative Council is dissolved;

Champion-7, the largest of its kind of oil-complex in Southeast Asia, is completed

1985 — The University of Brunei Darussalam opens with an enrollment of 176 students; Brunei National Democratic party (BNDP) is formed

1986 — Sultan Omar Ali Saifuddin dies

1987 — Brunei offers a $100,000,000 interest-free loan to Indonesia; the National Bank of Brunei closes; Malaysian prime minister Datuk Seri Dr. Mahathir Mohamad visits Brunei

1988 — Brunei and European Economic Community form a committee to look into joint business ventures; Brunei National Democratic party is dissolved by sultan; President Corazon Aquino of Philippines pays a state visit to Brunei

1989 — A memorandum is signed with the British government to purchase military equipment worth $472 million

1991 — The Sultan frees 6 political prisoners detained since an abortive revolt in 1962

IMPORTANT PEOPLE

Sultan Muda Hassanal Bolkiah (1946-   ), sultan since 1967; installed as crown prince in 1961 and coronated in 1968

James Brooke (1803-68), British adventurer, sailed in 1838 from India to Sarawak. He later became *rajah*, "ruler" of Sarawak.

Anthony Burgess (1917-   ), English novelist and critic; taught in Brunei, wrote *Devil of a State* (1961)

Joseph Conrad (1857-1924), Polish-born English novelist and short-story writer who wrote many stories about the Borneo area, like *Lord Jim* (1900)

Ferdinand Magellan (1480?-1521), Portuguese adventurer and sailor

Somerset Maugham (1874-1965), English fiction and drama writer, wrote stories about the Southeast Asia islands

Muhammad (A.D. 570?-632), prophet who founded the Islamic religion

Antonio Pigafetta (1481/1491?-1534), Portuguese sailor who chronicled Magellan's voyages to East Indies

Sultan Omar Ali Saifuddin (1916-86), sultan from 1950 to 1967, also minister of defense from 1984 to 1986

Boat landings at Bandar Seri Begawan

INDEX

Page numbers that appear in boldface type indicate illustrations

About the Author

David Wright was born and grew up in Richmond, Indiana. He first visited Southeast Asia while serving in the United States army in the Vietnam War.

Wright has spent more than ten years in newspapers as a reporter, copy editor, and editor. Newspapers range from *The Chicago Tribune* to the *Monroe* (Wisconsin) *Evening Times*.

Wright has written *Burma, Malaysia,* and *Vietnam* in the Enchantment of the World series. He has written five other books for Childrens Press, including the four-book series, *War in Vietnam*. He has written several books for adults.

He and his wife and two children live in West Bend, Wisconsin, forty miles northwest of Milwaukee. He has been a full-time, freelance writer, editor, and photographer for ten years.